Praise for *The Four Year Career®* *for Women* and Kimmy Brooke

"*The Four Year Career® for Women* is well done and greatly needed. Gives other women a heads up on their God Given greatness. It's fun to read a book and say 'Wish I had written this!'"

> – Rita Davenport, 20 Year President of Arbonne,
> Author and Speaker

"To win in this business, you have to think big and have a passion to change lives. This is who Kimmy is daily. Her book will awaken your potential and change your future."

> – Eric Worre, Founder of NetworkMarketingPro.com

"Network Marketing needs more tools made by and for women. I love *The Four Year Career®* and Kimmy's story is perfect to launch this new 'for women' version. Let Kimmy's fun personality and joyful spirit move you to take inspired action!"

> – Dr. Josephine Gross, Editor in Chief of *Networking Times*

"Kimmy Brooke is a shining example of the kind of heart, passion, authenticity and integrity that is essential for women to succeed in Network Marketing. Her story will inspire you, and her ideas will ignite your results and team growth."

> – Sonia Stringer, Speaker and Business Coach,
> Mentor to 400,000 women in Network Marketing

"You definitely want to devour this book ASAP. Kimmy knows how to make things happen in a major way when it comes to building a team. I meet a lot of people in my line of work as a network marketing trainer. Kimmy simply knows how to get it done. Read this now."

— Todd Falcone, Author, Speaker and Coach

.

"Definitely targeted to women but super mind expanding for anyone. Just finished reading this new book by my friend Kimmy Merrill Brooke. Anyone that wants to compress a forty year career into four and start living life NOW should read this!"

— Jordan Adler, Author of *Beach Money*

"Incredible book! Thank you Kimmy for sharing your gifts with us."

— Pamela Barnum, Top Earner, Speaker and Author

"The profession needed this book. It's fresh, unique, easy to read and will be a highly-effective business building tool no matter what company you're partnered with."

— Tommy Wyatt, Author, Speaker and Coach

"This book will help you define success on your own terms and achieve your entrepreneurial dreams."

— Dr. Dave Braun and Dr. Troy Amdahl, The Oola Guys

"Kimmy is a true professional and a leader to follow."

— Randy Gage, *New York Times* bestselling author of *Risky is the New Safe* and *Mad Genius*

THE FOUR YEAR CAREER® for women

FOURTH EDITION

put your future in YOUR own hands

or not...

KIMMY BROOKE

Published by Bliss Business.

For ordering information or special discounts for bulk purchases, please contact:

Bliss Business
1875 N. Lakewood Drive
Coeur d'Alene, ID 83814
(855) 480-3585
BlissBusiness.com
ISBN: 978-0-9979206-0-4

This book is dedicated to the two people in my life who move me daily.

For Hailey, the reason I said YES to my own Four Year Career.

For Richard, who truly is the wind beneath my wings.

CONTENTS

FOREWORD

I met Kimmy Merrill Everett in Houston, Texas, at The Mastermind Event. In a sea of 2,000 Network Marketing leaders from hundreds of companies around the world, she stood out even amongst this elite group. She was Joy, Love, Intensity and Optimism all bundled up in Beauty.

It pays to be nice to strangers. You never know who you are going to end up marrying. I didn't know it at the time, but she would soon be featured in my book *The Four Year Career*®, then we would date, fall in love, marry, and partner to help others build their own empires.

I wrote *The Four Year Career* after talking to thousands of people about building a second income in Network Marketing. It was not the products they objected to recommending, and it was certainly not a second income anyone was rejecting, but rather, the thought that it's "that kind of company" or a pyramid scheme. Decades of deceptive recruiting, hype, and empty promises left Network Marketing with a weak and ignorant reputation. I found success by teaching people about the beauty of the model, geometric progressions, and the asset value of a truly residual income.

The Four Year Career is just a story ... just an example of what is possible. It actually took me seven years to build mine, three to get my head around it, and four to get it done. Most people never get their heads around it. But Kimmy did. Without even having my book to inspire her, she built a team of 20,000 distributors in 12 countries in her first four years. And more importantly, she took people with her ... people who built their own second incomes and discovered that freedom may not be free ... but it is worth it.

As much as I would love to be able to think and write from a woman's perspective, I cannot. *The Four Year Career* is kind of a left-brain approach to understanding Network Marketing, an engineer's approach. I need to understand things before I believe in them. Some people are like me, and some people are like Kimmy. She prefers stories and inspiration, fun and humor to facts and mathematical formulas. And given that 80 percent of the people building empires in Network Marketing are women, she knew her version of the book would be of value. I agree.

We expect between the two of us—Mrs. Yin and Mr. Yang—you will have a much better shot of getting your head, and now your heart, around you being able to do this.

– Richard Bliss Brooke
Founder of Bliss Business, and author of
The Four Year Career® and *Mach2 With Your Hair on Fire*

INTRODUCTION

I wrote this book to support any woman who is adventurous enough to open it up and begin her journey to a richer, more fulfilling, and purpose-driven life. That is what a Four Year Career can offer you.

You may already be on your journey, and perhaps this read will enhance and accelerate your path. If you're anything like I was, you have no idea what THAT kind of life would look or feel like. Sound familiar? Then this book is definitely for you.

As you read my book, you may think of some friends who could benefit from the book as well. If so, please pass it on. Sharing is caring.

But first, let me rewind.

I met Richard Brooke at a conference in Houston, Texas, years ago. Out of all the people speaking, the things he shared made the most sense to me. It was from that meeting I learned about his book *The Four Year Career*®. His book is a great resource to help educate people about the model of Network Marketing and how it all works.

Ironically, I ended up marrying him, and we began a wonderful partnership in love, marriage, and business. As a team, we brainstorm, collaborate, and continuously think of ways to help more people understand what we do. It is from that place of inspiration that *The Four Year Career for Women* was born. I had an idea to share Richard's work in a more visual, feminine, hands-on experience. As a woman who created her own Four Year Career, who better to write the book than me?

The book is meant to be a quick, fun read that allows you to explore your life in a self-narrative, journaling type of way. You will have the opportunity to explore ideas, answer questions, and better understand the concept of this model we call Network Marketing. It will lead you to answer one simple question: *Is this for me?*

One last thing. While I call it a Four Year Career, results vary. Some build it in two years, others in 10, and others don't build anything at all. As you read, you will see the choice is yours. I look forward to your experience.

Go ahead ... pick up your pen, participate to your fullest, and enjoy the journey.

MY STORY

Once a Hawaii girl, always a Hawaii girl. Try as I might, I always ended up back on the island.

At age 40, I found myself living in paradise, newly divorced, financially strapped, and considering moving in with my mom. Working 60 plus hours a week did not allow for much more than getting my daughter, Hailey, to school on time, getting myself to the office, work, work, work, home to bed, and up the next day to do it all over again. I was grouchy, stressed out, and not much fun to be around. While I had a great job, it did not cover the Hawaii high cost of living.

Defining moments are meant to be just that. A moment in time where a realization hits you so hard you wonder how you never saw it before.

That moment came for me the day I took Hailey, 11 at the time, to the airport so she could spend the summer with her cousins and my sister in Colorado. While this may sound like a fun, wonderful experience, as a mom, it was heartbreaking. I watched my baby board the plane, knowing this would be the first time we would be separated. As I watched her turn the corner with elephant tears streaming down her face, I said to myself, "Enough is enough."

At that moment, I decided it was time for me to take control of my financial destiny. My sister had recently introduced me to the concept of Network Marketing. On that day I said, "I'm in." And in I was.

The only time I had to put into my new side business was during my lunch break. "An hour a day" became my motto, and my business began to grow quickly. Over the next four years, I created a team of nearly 20,000 people in 12 different countries.

I was able to quit a job I expected to be at for 15-20 more years of my life and start living the life my daughter and I longed for. At the same time, I've helped hundreds of other people begin to create their own Four Year Careers as well. Best of all, Hailey and I began to choose the places in the world we wanted to visit: Australia, Japan, Thailand, Indonesia, Singapore, Malaysia, Canada, the Bahamas, and many cities across the United States. She's never spent another holiday without me.

Financially, I've been able to use the income I earned in Network Marketing to create more assets through real estate investments. Hailey is now in college and I have been able to fully fund her education. To top it all off, I met and fell in love with an amazing man. He and I work together, play together, create together, and live a purpose-filled, passionate life on the Island of Lanai.

Together we own Bliss Business, a personal development, coaching, seminar, and Network Marketing tools and training business. We also build our own team in a Network Marketing company. Our vision is to educate and help tens of thousands of Network Marketers leave the profession and the world in a better place. A movement begins with just one person. Maybe that person is you, and that's why you are reading my book.

This could be your day one.

Chapter 1
Never Say Never

"Never say never because never is much further than you think."
                              - Kimmy Brooke

Have you ever caught yourself laughing at the fact that you are doing something you once said you would NEVER EVER do? Yup, I can relate! Some of the greatest things I've done, at one time in my life, have been on my NEVER EVER list. Isn't it interesting that we hold our opinions in each moment as FACT? When the reality is, they are just that. Opinions.

As we begin, let's take your current temperature on Network Marketing (AKA: Multi-Level Marketing, Direct Sales, Party Plans, "That Pyramid Thing").

Circle what's true for you:

What is Network Marketing?	Sounds Interesting	I'm Not Into "That"	I'm Willing To Get Educated

I can remember how Network Marketing received its stamp of approval from me when I learned that my sister Lisa (University of Colorado grad) and Katie, her sister-in-law (Stanford grad), had joined a company. I vividly recall thinking, "Well, if they're OK with doing it, so am I!" I won't deny I had a little voice in my head saying, "What will people think?" But that voice quickly disappeared when I received my first paycheck! From there, I began to educate myself on the validity of the profession.

I learned that 24 companies in Network Marketing are publicly traded on the Stock Market. I learned that many lawyers, doctors, principals, police officers, judges, and professional athletes are building businesses in Network Marketing. I learned that moms are able to stay home with their kids and build their careers right from their living rooms.

I learned that people like Warren Buffett, Robert Kiyosaki, and Tyra Banks all endorse and promote Network Marketing. In fact, Richard Branson himself said, "All the future jobs in the next 20 to 30 years will be created by Network Marketing entrepreneurs and other entrepreneurs around the world." I learned that many people are able to create an extra side income of $500 a month while others are able to create true financial freedom. Most importantly, I learned that my judgments and preconceived notions were flat-out wrong.

Okay, so what exactly is this Network Marketing thing?

Because products can't talk, they need someone to do the job for them. What better way to move a product than through people who love them? The model of Network Marketing allows the everyday person to become the voice and legs of a particular product or service. By sharing/selling this product or service with your network, you can gather customers and others who want to share and sell as well.

What makes this model so attractive is that instead of you, the individual, going out and selling a large amount of products yourself, you build a team of others who are doing the same, and in turn, you get paid a percentage on not only your own efforts, but on your team's efforts too. As your network of customers and distributors grows, so does your income.

There are thousands of companies to choose from and hundreds of people joining every day. Examples of some companies you may have heard of are Arbonne, Melaleuca, Mary Kay, Young Living, Stella & Dot, and LegalShield, to name a few.

In fact, check this out: Network Marketing produces more revenue ($183 billion a year) than the NFL ($13 billion), the film and entertainment industry ($88.3 billion), and global music sales ($15.7 billion) combined. *Source: World Federation of Direct Selling Association 2016 Report.

From what you circled as you started the book, you currently have a viewpoint about Network Marketing. Or maybe not. Remember, it's just your opinion. Are you open to the possibility of never saying never as well?

Chapter 2
4 vs 40

"I'd rather spend four years building MY dream than forty years building someone else's."
— *Kimmy Brooke*

Einstein called it the 8th Wonder of the World. Me, I call it the best-kept secret ... and I'm about to share it with you.

First, let's quickly check in:

Circle what's true for you right now:

I'm OK Financially	I Could Use A Financial Makeover	I Have Residual Income	I Don't Know What Residual Income Is	I Understand The Value of Compounding	Huh? Compounding? You Mean Like at The Pharmacy?

If you had asked me these questions in 2009, my overall answer would have been RUN. I was great at running away from my financial struggles, and the last thing I wanted to do was think about them!

From as far back as our Barbie-playing days, we are asked, "What do you want to be when you grow up?" A lawyer? A princess? A doctor? A mommy? Therefore, we move into the world with the idea of growing up and being something. With this notion comes the idea of going to school, doing well, getting good grades, getting into college, and ultimately, having a career. At least that's how it was for me. I did all those things. Well, maybe not always the "doing well" part, and before I could blink I was 40 years old.

The crazy thing was, at 40 I had nothing to show for all the years of hard work I'd put in over my life. Nothing. In fact, financially my life was such that even though I had a fabulous job, I was looking at moving in with my mom. Why?

Because I was forever on the 40+ career path. Work 40 hours

a week (60 in my case) for 40 years (again, more like 60 for me). If I had kept going at that pace, my retirement would have been feeble.

So here's a question for you. Are you currently happy with your financial situation? Or are you caught in the grind of the 40+ year career like I was? Or, maybe you don't have a career at all.

Let's take a look at where YOU are today, financially. If you're anything like I was, you may feel like putting the book down right now. I'm going to encourage you to KEEP GOING! I used to fly by the seat of my pants when it came to knowing where my money was being spent. I have to admit, the word "budget" has always made me cringe! Here's the great news. Becoming aware is the first step to creating more of what you want! The purpose of looking at where you are NOW financially is to help you see if more income would be valuable in your life. Let's take a glimpse at your current financial status. For the purpose of this exercise, only include YOUR income.

What I know to be true is that life can change in an instant. Something that may seem concrete and secure today (your spouse's income, alimony, child support) could very well NOT be tomorrow. I'd like to bring awareness to you of what you, yourself, are worth.

<u>Where are you now?</u>

Amount of income per month you bring home: _____

How much money is in your bank account that is yours?_____

How much of your money is disposable income
(spend on anything you want)? _____

How much money do you spend every month on:

Fun? _____

Clothes? _____

Travel? _____

Contributions? _____

How much money do you have left at the end of
the month? _____

If the answer is none, how much are you overspending
each month? _____

How much money would you LIKE to have left
each month? _____

Which defines your current situation best?

Awesome   **Shaky**   **Oh Boy**

How's that 40ish workin' so far?

OK, back to this best-kept secret leverage stuff.

For me, the idea of having MORE time on my hands and MORE
money in my pocket was a beautiful thought! *The Four Year
Career* allows just that.

The "L" word. Yup, that magic word. Leverage.

As an individual, we can only get paid on as many hours as we can work in a day. We call this trading hours for dollars. (i.e., I work 4 hours, I get paid x amount.)

But imagine having a group of 4 besties also each working 4 hours. You now have 20 vs 4 hours of work! That's leverage!

This eliminates the pressure cooker that "it's all on my shoulders," and instead creates a sense of "we're all in this together" because you grow a team.

Now, the magic in numbers.

Which would you rather have?

☐ A penny doubled every day for 30 days
☐ A million dollars cash right now

At first glance, a million dollars sounds pretty great, doesn't it? However, when you understand the power of compounding or geometric progression, a penny doubled every day for a month equals more than 5 million dollars! Yes, that's right. Those shiny little guys can become quite valuable!

Check this out. Day one isn't so exciting. You have a penny. Even at day 17, the doubling of the penny only equals $655. But soon enough the power of compounding sets in. When you continue to double that same penny over and over, by day 21 you have about $10,500. The very next day, day 22, you jump to almost $21,000. Things are starting to look pretty darn good. But wait. It gets even better. Day 26 doubles to $355,500, and day 27 goes to $670,000! Day 28 you become a millionaire, day 29 a double-digit millionaire, ending quite nicely on day 30 at over $5 million! Making sense? I hope you chose the penny over the $1 million to start! (Find a penny, pick it up.)

I had no idea these two concepts existed, and I did not understand someone like little old ME could easily have access to them. When I understood this model, I couldn't for the life of me get why the entire world wasn't jumping for joy about it! You, too, can have a Four Year Career, one that allows you access to leverage, compounding, and in turn, the residual income it will create.

Here you learn to build a team of friends who are all simply using and sharing a product or service on a regular basis. The bigger your team grows, the more products are being used and shared. The more products being used and shared, the bigger your income grows. It's that simple. (Reminder: I said simple, not easy. I'll get to that later.)

Let's have a little fun.

Thoughts ...

_____

_____

_____

_____

_____

_____

_____

Chapter 3
Oh the Possibilities

*"She's a dreamer, a doer, a thinker.
She sees possibility everywhere."*
                                    - unknown

Let's quickly reflect. As you started the book you got to lay out your current money situation.

<u>You decided if it was:</u>

Awesome   Shaky   Oh Boy

Maybe it looks better than you thought. Maybe not. Keeping this in mind, let's explore what your Four Year Career could look like. What would it feel like for you if you knew you could be in charge of your financial destiny?

| Amazing. Simply amazing. | Like 10,000 pounds has been lifted. | Tell me how NOW! | Nothing to write home about. |

How about a quick game of make believe? Remember your 4 besties who helped you understand the "L" word (Leverage)? Let's see what happens when you start to share ice cream with them. First, who are some of your besties?

Go ahead and fill in the first 4 names that come to your mind.

BFF 1: _____

BFF 2: _____

BFF 3: _____

BFF 4: _____

The great thing about women is we all have different friends from different circles. So your besties will most likely have other besties in addition to you! Once you fill in their names, scroll through the drawing to see what happens as you and your BFFs start spreading the ice cream love.

As a note, there are as many different pay structures as there are companies. Generally, you can expect to be paid an average of 7 percent of your sales. This example is modeled on that percentage.

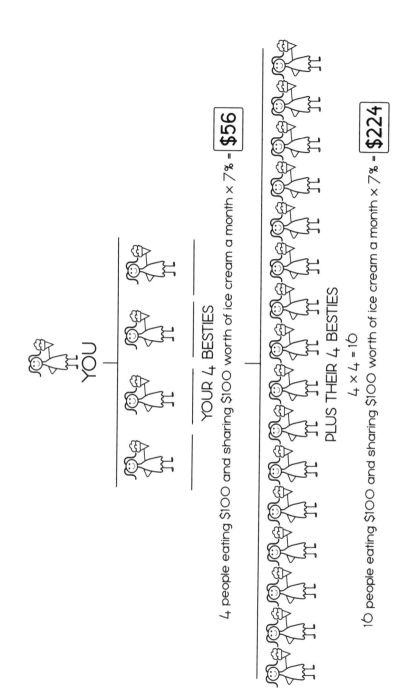

YOU

YOUR 4 BESTIES

4 people eating $100 and sharing $100 worth of ice cream a month × 7% = **$56**

PLUS THEIR 4 BESTIES

4 × 4 = 16

16 people eating $100 and sharing $100 worth of ice cream a month × 7% = **$224**

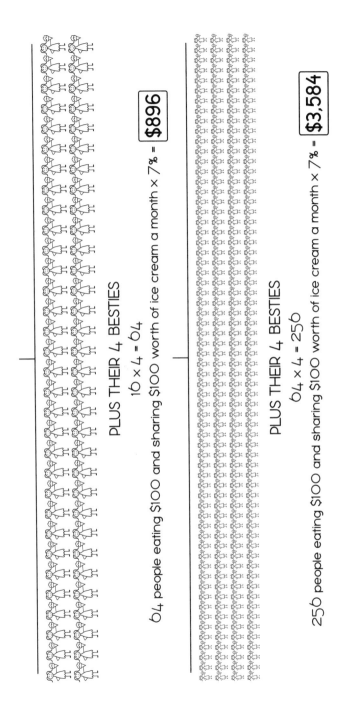

PLUS THEIR 4 BESTIES
16 × 4 = 64

64 people eating $100 and sharing $100 worth of ice cream a month × 7% = **$896**

PLUS THEIR 4 BESTIES
64 × 4 = 256

256 people eating $100 and sharing $100 worth of ice cream a month × 7% = **$3,584**

The geometric equation: 4 grows to 16 grows to 64 grows to 256 grows to ???? It's really up to you where it goes from there. Let your imagination go and dream big. Remember, all this because you said yes and shared with 4.

At first glance, it may not look too exciting when just you, your four BFFs, and their BFFs are eating and sharing the scoops. The magic happens when your team grows for several years, when you have people all over the country—even the globe—using and sharing. This is when the compounding sets in just like when you double the penny.

This is why it's called the Four Year Career (not the Four Week or Four Month Career). Like a great bottle of wine, it gets better with time! With time, this tasty treat is an asset called Residual Income ... money that continues to pay you over and over and over.

In this example, you've earned almost $5,000 of income monthly. You have built an asset that, if you were to take it to the bank, would be worth a million dollars. Now, just consider how long it would take and how much it would cost to build any other asset worth $1 million (real estate, stocks, or interest on cash in the bank).

*Disclaimer: I am not insinuating people will eat and share $200 worth of ice cream every month. This is merely a generic, silly, and fun example of what is possible as geometric progression kicks in. Not every person on the drawing will find four friends and customers. In fact, many will quit before they ever even have the chance to see the geometric progression go to work. Now that we got the disclaimer out of the way, let's get back to you!

Remember this question from earlier...

How much money would you LIKE to have left each month? (page 13)

Keeping this in mind, and using the example of sharing ice cream, what kind of income would bring a smile to your face in:

(Remember we are playing make believe. You can reach for the stars here.)

6 months? _____
2 Years?   _____
4 Years?   _____

Jot down a few things here you would do with this extra cabbage. Think big!

_____

_____

_____

_____

_____

Cool. Now we will look at what it takes to make this happen and see if you are up for the challenge.

Chapter 4
The Ins and Outs

*"And suddenly you know ... It's time to
start something new and trust the magic
of beginnings."*

— unknown

So, how does someone DO this?

Here's the lowdown. Every company has its own method of building the Four Year Career. What's great is the core activities are pretty much the same ... when you actually do them.

The basics:
1. Be a customer of the product yourself—duh. Who would want to promote stuff they don't like?
2. Build a list of friends, family, coworkers, everyone you want to share your business and products with. The bigger you build this list, the BETTER.
3. Invite friends to take a look at what you are doing.
4. Share your products and business with them.

5. Allow them to decide:
    a. I would like to be a customer.
    b. I would like to lock arms and build a business with you.
    c. It's not for me.
    d. I would like to think about it.
       (Sharing *The Four Year Career®* and *The Four Year Career® for Women* can help them decide too.)

Each company has a system and training to teach you, which you will receive when you join. The person who introduced you to the business becomes your sponsor, and they will be working with you to support you in your success. If you and your sponsor start at the same time, you will get support from the leaders in your team. As your team grows, you will begin to teach and train them as well. Not to worry. Learn as you earn is the motto here.

You do not need to prepare yourself for months, study until you're blue in the face, or pass a test to get started in Network Marketing. Yes, there will be a little bit of training you will want to do on day one so you know how your company does business. Most of your training and learning, however, will occur as you "do."

It's like riding a bike. The only way you learn how to ride a bike is by riding it. Someone can tell you how to jump on the bike and someone can tell you what it feels like as you ride, but you won't actually know until you, yourself, get on the bike and experience it firsthand.

The same goes here. Until you make that very first invitation to that very first bestie, you won't know exactly how to do it. So the best thing is: JUST DO IT!

As every company has its own way, I'm not going to get too deep into details. You will get up to speed when/if you join. However, I'll share a few helpful, quick tips here from one woman to another since you've come this far.

1. Your vibe attracts your tribe. And trust me, you want to work with a tribe of awesome women (and men of course). Showing up as your best, you will bring other awesome peeps to your team. Don't be desperate to enroll EVERYONE. Invite people you would love to work with to look at your business.

2. Trust. Throw out the "I'll do it my way" song you may be used to singing. Trust those who have had the success. Let them coach you to yours. We call this being coachable! Don't try to reinvent the wheel.

3. Listen. When you listen, you learn a lot about the person you are talking to. Instead of doing all the talking, learn to listen and ask questions that will help you understand what's important for the friend you are sharing with.

4. Honor people. If you want to create a special business, always honor people and put your friendships first. By respecting people when they tell you no (yes, people will tell you no), you will in turn get respect back. *More on "no's" in the next chapter.

5. Consistency. A little bit every day is far better than nothing at all.

I found the learning curve to be quick in comparison to other professions. Just like when riding that bike, you remember what NOT to do by stumbling. Mistakes can be your best teacher, so you don't need to be perfect as you begin. More important is the decision that you are up for the challenge.

Chapter 5
Mary, Mary,
Quite Contrary

"Sometimes the smallest step in the right direction ends up being the biggest step of your life. Tip toe if you must, but take the step."

– unknown

I'm not saying the Four Year Career is easy. In fact, because most of us are used to immediate gratification, it's challenging for many to be patient enough to allow the compounding of a Four Year Career to kick in. Some will even quit just a day before that could have happened for them. Imagine that. Probably the biggest challenge is people will say no. Not everyone gets this model. And that's okay. Many have an inaccurate idea of what it is. That is why my husband wrote *The Four Year Career* and why I wrote this book.

But for every four or so no's, there may be a yes right around the corner. You will find someone who also wants to change her financial future, and because you said yes, you get to show her how. So, you get to decide if you're up to the task. For me, there was no other answer. I could handle all the no's in the world if I could somehow create freedom for my daughter and myself.

Think about a beautiful garden. As you start growing your garden, you till, you mulch, you plant your seeds. Consistently you water the garden, weed the garden, and love on it. If you don't water every day, the seeds will not sprout. Some days may be very dry and require more effort. You cannot neglect this fragile environment as it begins to flourish, and you definitely cannot afford to stop paying attention to it because life gets in the way. Once you plant your seeds, there's no turning back. You are all in, or the flowers and plants will not make it.

Your Four Year Career has the chance to become your beautiful garden. But only if you're willing to put the consistent effort in. You cannot expect it to grow on its own. You need to nurture it, pay attention to it, and give it your focus until it gets to a place where it is ripe and blooming, full of fruits for you to harvest! Just like in your garden, there will be surprises and unknowns. Some veggies won't make it. Some will produce only one or two pieces of fruit. You will have people who say they want to build something who don't. You will have many who just want to use your products and never build a team. But it only takes one seed to grow a giant vine of beautiful ripe tomatoes!

What will your garden look like? Will you be diligent enough to water, weed, and love on your garden so you reap the fruits of your labor? If so, LET'S GET PLANTING!

Chapter 6
I Am Super Woman, Hear Me Roar

"When your life is on course with its purpose, you are your most powerful."
– Oprah

Are you asking yourself *but can I really do this?* I get it. I asked myself the same question. I believe YOU have great value to offer the world. Possibly value you don't see in yourself. Yet.

Sometimes we overlook, dismiss, or even forget our many talents. The beauty here in Network Marketing is every single thing you have done has led you right to this moment. Everything you've done has value! Even your mistakes!

You have a treasure chest of gifts, and we are going to celebrate them here! Let's take some time to get all your attributes down on paper. These attributes will serve you well in your Four Year Career. Really, the most important key to success here is that you like people. Everything else can be learned! Let's see how many talents you already possess that will serve you well in the arena of building a Four Year Career.

Mom of _____ kids

Married _____ years

Places I've lived: _____

_____

Sports I've played: _____

I've been a team captain: _____

Schools I've attended: _____

I have degree(s) in: _____

Places I've traveled: _____

All the jobs I've had: _____

My worst job ever: _____

Teams I've coached: _____

I am/was a class mom: _____

Boards I've served on: _____

Committees I've participated in: _____

Causes I've participated in: _____

I'm passionate about: _____

I'm best at: _____

Check what's applicable for you:

☐ I have close relationships with my friends
☐ I'm funny
☐ I'm shy
☐ I keep my word (show up on time, do what I say I will do)
☐ I love writing
☐ I love reading books
☐ I love learning new things
☐ I love math
☐ I love shopping
☐ I love cooking
☐ I love speaking
☐ I love teaching
☐ I love coordinating

Add as many more things as you can think of here: _____

_____

_____

_____

_____

_____

_____

_____

_____

_____

For a moment, take in this list of all the things you have done and accomplished. Believe it or not, every single skill you have will somehow translate into a strength for your Four Year Career. You may not know how that love/hate PTA position will benefit you, so let me tell you. As the head of the PTA, you organized, planned, and inspired others to follow your vision. That gives you a head start to leading a team. Not to mention you have all those other PTA parents to add to your list of people to share your business with! I never imagined that steering a canoe for years as a kid would benefit me in my business. What it gave me was the know-how to inspire and motivate, two fabulous skills used in Network Marketing.

So go ahead and give yourself a hug. Heck, while you're at it, look in the mirror. And repeat after me. (Yes, out loud.)

"I am Super Woman, hear me roar. I have talents and skills to rock this thing."

Again, but louder.

"I am Super Woman, hear me ROAR. I am totally awesome!"

And again.

"I AM SUPER WOMAN, HEAR ME ROAR. I CAN DO ANYTHING I CHOOSE TO DO!"

Thoughts ...

_____

_____

_____

_____

_____

_____

_____

Chapter 7
It's in Our DNA

"She believed she could, so she did."
– R.S. Grey

Did you know that as women we were actually BORN to excel as Network Marketers? From as far back as our gathering days, women have thrived on building community, collaboration, sharing, storytelling, and helping others ... all the essential skills used here. When was the last time you recommended something to a friend? Probably today. And yet, sometimes we get stuck when it comes to building a Four Year Career around the idea that we "can't sell to our friends."

Circle what's true for you:

Had a Party	Put the Kids to Bed	Gotten a Job	Been Asked Out on a Date	Gotten Married

If you answered YES to one or more of these, guess what? YOU CAN SELL. Selling doesn't mean badgering. Selling doesn't mean hounding. Selling simply means sharing something you are passionate about with the people you care for in your life because you believe what you have can help them. That's not such a bad thing, now is it?

And how about that multitasking? There are mixed reviews out there about doing many things at once, but we know multitasking is absolutely in a woman's DNA. Without this God-given skill, we wouldn't be able to pull off all the amazing things we do as women! We wouldn't be able to feed the kids, answer the phone, check the homework, and do the dishes, all while walking the dog.

We have the gift of wearing many hats. The great thing about the Four Year Career is you can wear this hat alongside all the other hats you already have. It doesn't have to become your only hat. It can remain a part of your repertoire just like your Mom hat, Corp. Exec hat, Wife hat, and Friend hat. You simply make more room on the hat rack. Watch out, Four Year Career hat coming through!

Fill in the hats you wear…

Mom
Wife
Friend
Professional
Coach
Counselor
Party planner
Chauffeur
Chef

You may be thinking … "Look at all my hats. I already wear so many!" I get it! I was there. Working 60 plus hours a week, being solely responsible for my daughter, putting food on the table, getting Hailey to her sports, and helping with her homework left very little me time. The thought of one more thing seemed daunting, until I saw the bigger picture. When I realized THIS hat was the ticket to actually get me out of my overwhelm, I decided I could squeeze that extra hour in each day and it would be worth it. The question to ask yourself is this:

How much time COULD I have each day to help myself get closer to my list of things I want?

Circle what's true for you:

30 minutes	1 hour	2 hours	No Time At All

If you were able to circle anything but "no time at all," you have enough time to start creating your Four Year Career. Sorry to say, if your answer was "no time at all," now is not the right time for you to add another hat to your life. Perhaps things will shift for you in the future, and you can dust this book off and reread then. Onward we charge.

Let's look at one last piece. Money. We were born to have it. We were meant to live in abundance, not struggle. We were meant to thrive, enjoy, create, give, support, and shine! A common truth in the world is this: It takes money to make money. So yes, it will cost you a start-up fee to begin your Four Year Career, just as it would cost you to start a small business, buy a franchise, or become a doctor, lawyer, designer, or musician.

Expecting it to be any different in this profession would be silly. But the great news is, in comparison to almost every other business out there, the start-up cost is quite low. Every company is different, but you can expect some sort of starting fee to become a distributor. I invite you now to scroll back to page 23 of the besties and all that ice cream and look at what your potential is financially.

Thoughts ...

Chapter 8
Home Sweet Home

"There's no place like home."
- Dorothy, The Wizard of Oz

OK, I'm feeling it. Where do I begin?

There are thousands of companies to choose from when joining the Network Marketing profession. Just like choosing the right pair of shoes, when you are looking to choose your home, you want to make sure it fits YOU.

A quick checklist:

☐ Make sure you love the product(s) you will represent. It will be challenging to build a Four Year Career promoting products you are not passionate about.

☐ Does the company you are looking at align with your values? Do some online research. Do the owners, leaders, and team members resonate with your beliefs?

☐ Does the company have a support system to help you succeed?

☐ Who will you be working with? (We call this your Upline.) Do you align with who they are? Do you want to hang out with them, take trips with them, and have them around your family?

☐ Give yourself a gut check. Does your intuition tell you this is the right home?

If you have red flags about anything, don't hesitate to ask! Get your questions answered. Choose a company that supports your interests and passions. Here's a start to help you brainstorm.

I'm interested in:

☐ Health & Wellness	☐ Jewelry
☐ Travel	☐ Solar Power
☐ Skin Care	☐ Cellular
☐ Makeup	☐ Legal Services
☐ Candles	☐ Life Insurance
☐ Weight Loss	☐ Dental Insurance
☐ Exercise	☐ Essential Oils
☐ Greeting Cards	☐ Gifts

Keeping in mind what you love and could easily promote, you can start doing some digging to see which companies could be a fit for you. If a friend shared this book with you, they are probably in a company, and that would be the best place for you to start your research. Regardless, home is where the heart is, and you want to be sure your heart is in the right place to get a great start.

Thoughts ...

_____

_____

_____

_____

_____

Chapter 9
And the Boxing Gloves Come Off

"When women come together with a collective intention, magic happens."
– Phylicia Rashad

Can you remember the last time you heard a girlfriend gossiping ... saying things that just weren't nice? I imagine it wasn't too long ago. Am I right? Guess what? I have a secret for you. If they are gossiping TO you, I would be willing to bet they are also gossiping about you. I call it MGS. Mean Girl Syndrome. And it stinks.

When I joined the Network Marketing profession, I felt this "whispering" behind my back. It got back to me (as gossip usually tends to do) that my "friends" were saying all sorts of silly judgmental remarks about my choices. Sometimes change terrifies people, and my friends saw me changing. Gossiping was their way of feeling better about themselves.

One of the most remarkable, beautiful gifts I have received from this profession is forming relationships with a different kind of woman. A different kind of friendship. A different way of being. It may sound too good to be true, but I want you to know it's not. Women in Network Marketing are evolved.

The concept of competition is replaced with the ideal of collaboration, and instead of telling secrets about each other, you learn here how to support, encourage, and champion each other. What you have to look forward to is connection with women in a healthy, beautiful way.

You get the opportunity to grow deep relationships with women you most likely would never have met outside the profession. But because you got started in your Four Year Career, you find yourself surrounded by women who care about you; women who don't tolerate pettiness and gossip; women who are loving and looking out for your best interest. Can you imagine a community (a large one at that) of women who have your back? Well, take a nice big deep breath because the gloves are off.

In addition to meeting great women in your own company, you will also meet women throughout the profession who inspire you, teach you, and become some of your very best friends. I still love my non-networking friends. Gossip and all. But I have deeper, more meaningful relationships with the women I work with. Together we discuss big ideas. Big dreams. Big visions. And together we help to make them come true.

In fact, it's even bigger than just you and the women who lift you up here. Women across the Network Marketing profession have united for a powerful cause to change the lives of women worldwide. Together, we are aiming to be a part of the biggest shift in human history. Women United for Change is a movement in partnership with Project Concern International (PCI) to create peace and prosperity on our planet by economically empowering women. To see the many women involved in this movement, go to **womenunitedforchange.com**. Believe it or not, just by reading this book you have helped to empower another woman's life as well. Hats off to you!

This is certain. Big things happen when women come together. An unimaginable ripple is created. By saying YES, you join this movement and surround yourself in support, community, and love. Move over gossip, it's time to empower one another.

Chapter 10
If Nothing Changes,
Nothing Changes

*"Make a choice to take a chance
or your life will never change."*
                                    – unknown

The truth about life is, if you keep doing the same thing over and over, there is no question you WILL get the same results. During this read, you've had a chance to get honest with yourself about where you currently stand financially. My guess is if you're anything like most of us out there, you could use a boost in the $ department. Heck, even when you're at the top of your game, who doesn't want more?

You've also had a quick glimpse into a doorway of a new path. I get it. Sometimes doing something new, outside the box, and possibly even misunderstood by others, can be scary. The alternative is to stay where you are and be OK with it.

Eleanor Roosevelt said, "You must do the thing you think you cannot do." I like that chica. When I got started, I was looking to make an additional $500 a month so I could pay my rent. I didn't read a book, see a presentation, or do any research. I jumped in with both feet and started running. I worked tirelessly for years to build my asset, and it paid off.

While the income has profoundly changed my life, I feel it is only one of oh-so-many benefits I never realized I would receive from this career. I would have to say the biggest cherry on top for me has been the freedom I have. I get to choose when I work, and when I play. I get to play a lot. I get to play a lot with people I didn't know, but now do, because of this career: women with like minds; women who like to talk about meaningful things and do meaningful things.

I get to see my daughter whenever I want. At any moment, I can hop on a plane to visit her or she can fly home to see me. I can take a nap during the day or stay up until 3 a.m. watching movies because I work for me and only me. I've been able to set an example for my daughter that even in the toughest of circumstances, you can make choices that bring you what you deserve as long as you're willing to work for it. I have become a better me, and in turn, the world is a little bit better.

So what would bring peace and joy to you?

☐ More self-love
☐ A beautiful relationship
☐ Time to travel
☐ Money to make a difference in other's lives
☐ More time with your family
☐ New community of friends
☐ Stretching yourself and becoming your best you
☐ Building a legacy for your children
☐ Empowering other women
☐ Wealth

You name it; it's all right here waiting for you to grab.

What if you knew for certain that in the next four years you could have an asset? An asset that over time, paid you every month regardless if you worked or not. An asset that you created all on your own, that belonged to you and only you. An asset that you could share with whomever you wanted. An asset that helped you get all the things in life you dream about, think about, and wish for. Is there anything or anyone that could stop you from going for it?

I know this: If you DECIDE you can do this, you can. You have the ability to be one of the stories in the back of this book. (Turn to page 82 and see.) There's nothing I would love more. I believe you can make this happen.

The only question left is ... DO YOU?

Four Year
Career Women

*"She not only saw a light at the end of the
tunnel, she became that light for others."*
                                        – unknown

SUCCESS STORIES

The following stories feature people who may be much like you. Certainly in the beginning, they didn't understand or necessarily believe in the possibilities of Network Marketing. And as you will read, most were not instant successes. Many of them have the same stories as most people during their first few months or even years ... "This doesn't work!"

Yet, if you can reflect on the examples of duplication, compounding, and tending to your garden, it might help you make sense of these massive success stories. This is a much bigger opportunity than most people believe. And that is the promise of Network Marketing ... that it is just an opportunity. What you do with it is up to you. These stories are a sample of people I know who have made it big in Network Marketing and did it in an ethical and responsible manner in companies of the same character.

DISCLAIMER

These success stories are exceptional exceptions and are shared here to inspire you and show you people from different walks of life who have succeeded. They are not what you should expect to accomplish. They are 1 out of 10,000 or less. And yet it is interesting to note where they came from and what they accomplished. And maybe, just maybe, you could do the same.

The Four Year Career Women

Seeing is believing. It was once said that "storytelling is the most powerful way to see ideas put into action."

Each of these super women has her own unique story. Some were not necessarily looking for change, and others were desperate for it. Some had money, but no time to be with their families. Others had time, but no money to pursue their passions and dreams.

Yet, they all share a single common bond. They found true freedom through this amazing model we call Network Marketing.

My hope is that these stories will leap off the page and speak to you; that they'll light a fire within and show you what's possible ... for YOU.

And success in Network Marketing is just that ... a possibility. Most people never do much with the opportunity. But for those who DO, their lives are forever changed and filled with rich, cherry-on-top moments.

Dig in.

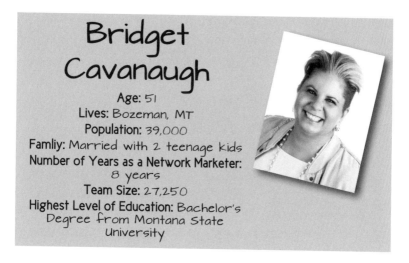

Bridget Cavanaugh

Age: 51
Lives: Bozeman, MT
Population: 39,000
Famliy: Married with 2 teenage kids
Number of Years as a Network Marketer: 8 years
Team Size: 27,250
Highest Level of Education: Bachelor's Degree from Montana State University

Before: Director of Marketing for a start-up software company

Old Annual Income: $110,000

The Old Me: Even at the top of my career game, I was professionally fatigued, asking myself daily, is this all there is? Burnout was inevitable and secretly welcomed. I had done it all, yet a sense of purpose and fulfillment eluded me. Little did I know that epic life changes were just one conversation away..

My Four Year Career:

Looking For It / (Found Me)

My new career took me by total surprise. In a matter of minutes, I went from "maybe" to "must do." I shocked my doubts with action and enrolled instantly.

How I Heard of Network Marketing: My understanding of Network Marketing was completely an inside job, meaning I didn't know anything about it until I made a go of it. I learned on the job, and in many ways, I am still learning and fine-tuning my approach.

Move Over Ice Cream, Let's See the Real Deal:

YEAR ONE: Year one was the "year of habits." I set a part-time business routine that would allow me to enroll 2-3 business partners a month and 4 customers consistently. At the end of my first year, I had recruited nearly 22 new partners and 26 customers. This resulted in 100 business builders, putting the entire organization at 1,000+.

YEAR TWO: This was the "year of proof." A six-figure income was inevitable, and so was retirement from my 24-year career. Team culture of performance and purpose was taking shape. At the end of the year, our team of business builders was 300+.

YEAR THREE: Year three was the "year of the warrior." I was now fully retired and free to own my time. I spent it pushing the limits of what I thought was possible. My biggest recruiting year, I was number one in the fastest growing team in the company with 50 new partners joining me and more than 1,800 business builders.

YEAR FOUR: My husband and I call this the "year of scalable by design." New leaders were taking charge of big teams, building their own cultures around giving and serving. We didn't have to hand the baton, they eagerly stepped into their greatness. At this point, we were 5,500 strong in every town, city, and state across the US.

Who I've Become: I've become wholehearted and confident in who I am. I won't lie, I leaned on my competitive nature and compared and hustled my way through the first three years, but this gave way to gratitude and personal growth. My purpose of "championing the dreams of others" began to come into focus. I had a gift and wanted to use it wisely.

Because I Said Yes, I Now: Every person whose self-belief I elevated or hopefulness I instilled, is a huge victory. This is where legacies begin: not in explosive events, but in the daily practice and culture of greatness that gets passed from person to person. I've been able to raise big funds and give big donations to organizations I'm passionate about. Giving should scale along with your business, and that too will duplicate.

Cherry on Top Moments:

- My kids' reaction the first day I started working from home.
- The day my husband officially joined me in business and we could call this a "partnership" and not just "my wife's business."
- Maui, Paris, Bangkok, London, Sydney, Cancun: all places I never could have afforded to travel to before.
- The brilliant moment team members who joined after me exceeded my earnings.

From One Woman to Another: Be authentic and vulnerable even as your fame and freedom grow. Share your struggles, share your secrets, and be abundant with the ups and downs of your journey. Every day, I make sure people see the ordinary person, the strengths and the faults. If I can be real and approachable, and make success in this business feel accessible and doable by everyone, then I've done my job well, and you will too.

April Pointer

Age: 42
Lives: Frisco, TX
Population: 100,000
Famliy: Married with 2 kids
Number of Years as a Network Marketer: 7 years
Team Size: 750,000+
Highest Level of Education: Bachelor's of Science in Nutrition and Food Science

Before: I was a successful nutritionist. When we started our family, I decided to stay at home and be a homeschool mom.

Old Annual Income: $50,000

The Old Me: We were really deep in debt due to a medical issue I have had since birth. This debt consumed us. While my husband worked hard all day, I focused on raising the kids, and did little side jobs like running an organic food co-op. I was painfully frugal, yet creative in order to live the healthy lifestyle I desired for our family.

My Four Year Career:

Looking For It   / (Found Me)

I was solely a product user for two years. Everything changed when a friend asked me to teach her circle of friends about the product. I was shocked I could get paid for sharing something this GOOD.

How I Heard of Network Marketing: I learned of the industry in college when I joined an MLM company based on the opportunity alone. I was focused on my education and didn't do the income-producing activities to grow anything. I eventually quit. Ten years later I was introduced to my company, but got in for the product, not the opportunity. Two years later, I agreed to teach a class for a friend. After making several hundred dollars at that first meeting, my eyes were opened that THIS could be the key to erasing years of medical debt, while helping people get healthy.

Move Over Ice Cream, Let's See the Real Deal:

YEAR ONE: I worked this part time, as my focus was homeschooling. I taught friends and their friends about the product and enrolled 2-3 people a month.

YEAR TWO: Duplication started to take off, and I created a $30,000 annual income. I continued to enroll 2-3 people a month and my team did the same. I began to grow in my personal development.

YEAR THREE: My husband was laid off and I suddenly switched from part-time to full-time mode. He joined me in the business, and we created a six-figure annual income and an organization of 21,000 members.

YEAR FOUR: I did everything my mentors said to do. In turn, I reached the top rank and six figures monthly vs. annually! The organization grew to 250,000 members.

Who I've Become: I am more confident and know how to push through fears instead of letting them paralyze me. #fearchaser. I made it a habit to get out of my comfort zone and into my courage zone. I've learned to never commit to anything you lack passion in. Why? Because you'll find yourself overwhelmed by saying yes to too many things that aren't associated with your own dream.

Because I Said Yes, I Now: As a little girl always hospitalized, I dreamed of being in a profession where I could help people be healthy. I now get to inspire thousands via our product and business opportunity. Legacy is the word God gave our family as our life mantra. We want to make a HUGE difference in the world by leaving a legacy of goodness. My husband and I now give to 26 organizations. This brings us so much JOY!

Cherry on Top Moments:

- My kids watching me chase my dreams (so they in turn will chase theirs) and creating a legacy for them.
- Getting 100 percent out of debt and paying cash for our cars.
- Giving away multiple cars to single moms in need.
- Finding my tribe; the friends that are truly going to be lifelong ... and rallying with them to achieve their own dreams!
- Traveling the world with my whole family in tow 100 percent of the time.

From One Woman to Another: Respect your own time and happiness enough to choose the type of leadership role that plays to YOUR strengths, YOUR gifts, and YOUR passion. Commit to put what you learn into action. One person's courage to step out and do this can impact a million people around the world: the butterfly effect. Honor yourself with your work because your earning power is DIRECTLY related to your commitment.

Twice As Nice

Jenifer Furness

Age: 46
Lives: Davenport, IA
Population: 99,700
Famliy: Married with 2 kids
Number of Years as a Network Marketer: 5 years
Team Size: 2,900
Highest Level of Education: BS in Occupational Therapy, BA in Psychology

Jeanie Fountain

Age: 46
Lives: Bettendorf, Iowa (Quad Cities)
Population: 34,200
Famliy: Married with 4 kids
Number of Years as a Network Marketer: 5 years
Team Size: 1,478
Highest Level of Education: BS in Occupational Therapy, BA in Psychology

Before: We were both Occupational Therapy Managers

Old Annual Income: $100,000+

The Old Us: We were "successful" occupational therapy managers, devoting 18 years of our lives to our careers. We dropped our kids off at daycare since they were 6 weeks old, worked 50+ hours/week, and were always tired.

Our Four Year Career:

Looking For It / Found Us

We were always entrepreneurial, looking for ways to be our own "bosses," but always landed in the brick and mortar of traditional business. We were never taught anything but employee and business owner mindsets. We didn't see Networking Marketing as a true "profession" and definitely never imagined it would be the answer to our prayers!

How We Heard of Network Marketing: Jenifer: I was introduced via a "random" Facebook post, and after a few months of compelling results, I demanded my twin sister's credit card, because who wants to do anything new and exciting without her best friend?!

Move Over Ice Cream, Let's See the Real Deal:

YEAR ONE: Jenifer: I personally sponsored 10 people in the first year and Jeanie sponsored 5. We were both car qualified and determined to create more success for our teams. Our OT company closed that year, and I pushed ahead into Network Marketing while Jeanie chose the job route. My husband gave me an ultimatum of "two months to make this successful or you're getting a 'real' job." I won.

YEAR TWO: Jenifer: I personally sponsored 2 more people and Jeanie 3. Jeanie cut her hours to part-time while I "burned the ships" and gave up my license to practice OT. I was all in!

YEAR THREE: Jeanie: I joined Jenifer in "retirement." We continued sprinting together and both of our businesses grew tremendously … to the top of the company!

YEAR FOUR: We both sponsored 2 more business partners each and drove depth in our teams. Driving depth to reach our goals rather than sponsoring hundreds personally has been effective on our road to success.

Who We've Become: Looking back over the last 4 years, our transformations physically, emotionally, financially, and even spiritually have been staggering! Through personal development, we've become better wives, better mothers, and better human beings. We spent nearly two decades believing our careers were the only way to provide. Now, we realize more than ever, true success and fulfillment are discovered in service to others. Our ability to make an impact in the world has grown exponentially through this great profession.

Because We Said Yes, We Now: We have declared to feed 1 million children by 2020 as our WHY and mission. We support World Vision & Compassion International, and we are key sponsors to local charities and missions for children and families in need. So many kids go to school in our own back yards without socks and underwear! Unacceptable—we will make a difference.

Cherry on Top Moments:

- Retiring our husbands.
- Setting the example for our kids and grandkids that our envisioned lives drive our real lives. As Earl Nightingale declared, "We become what we think about…" Powerful!
- True freedom and flexibility to spend time with our kids and family traveling the world—no longer living paycheck to paycheck. Heck, we never even had a passport until this great industry taught us to dream again!
- A stronger faith in God, compelling us to give back and pay it forward.

From One Woman to Another: If your current life is not taking you to your dream life, MOVE! As Jim Rohn always said, "You're NOT a tree!" Life is too short to live in black and white … true purpose and fulfillment are only found in FULL COLOR! Other people's blessings are tied to our obedience! What are you waiting for?

This success story is not typical. It is an exceptional exception shared here to inspire you and show you what's possible. It is not what you should expect to accomplish.

Aldis Loreno

Age: 54
Lives: Saratoga Springs, NY and Orlando, FL
Population: 27,000 and 255,000
Famliy: 2 adult daughters
Number of Years as a Network Marketer: 11 years
Team Size: 50,000+
Highest Level of Education: BA in Politics

Before: Real Estate Broker

Old Annual Income: $150,000+

The Old Me: I was a successful real estate broker, and although I enjoyed it, I worked A LOT. I was at the mercy of my clients and worked days, evenings, weekends, and holidays because it was convenient for them. Juggling that career and my girls in high school was a struggle. They were leaving for college in two years, and I wanted to be able to help pay for their education without putting us into a ton of debt.

My Four Year Career:

Looking For It / (Found Me)

Initially skeptical of the Network Marketing industry, I realized that this company was going to do well with or without me. I didn't want to be kicking myself later for letting my ego get in the way, so I jumped in, and it was the best decision I've ever made.

How I Heard of Network Marketing: A colleague called and asked me to try the products. Out of respect, I agreed, but when she started talking to me about doing it as a business, I thought it all sounded too good to be true, and to be totally honest, I thought I was too good for it. I was worried about what people would think. Ultimately, I didn't let that stand in my way because when I finally did some homework, I realized what a brilliant business model this was.

Move Over Ice Cream, Let's See the Real Deal:

YEAR ONE: I worked it part time alongside my real estate business, but I was very business-focused. I sponsored 10 people and concentrated on helping the ones who really "wanted it." That got our team to the "car" level in 7 months.

YEAR TWO: I personally sponsored around 10 new business partners. By month 20 I reached the top level, and at that point, I was making way more money in Network Marketing than in my real estate career. I emptied out my real estate desk and starting working my Network Marketing business full time.

YEAR THREE: and FOUR: I personally sponsored 10 people, and my team grew to over 8,000 members by year four. I now have an organization of superstars (many are better than I'll ever be), and I'm proud to be their business "granny." After 11 years, the growth keeps going. My team is now over 50,000 strong!

Who I've Become: I've become a confident and independent woman. By pushing through my initial fears and hesitations, not only have I achieved what I wanted for myself and my family, but for so many other families as well. The domino effect is fantastic! Getting out of our comfort zones makes us feel courageous and proud, and by going first and leading the way, we open the door for so many others.

Because I Said Yes, I Now: I have been able to donate to Alzheimer's and dementia-related research organizations. Both my grandmother and aunt passed away from Alzheimer's disease, and the impact on our family and all others dealing with it was devastating. I am also an avid supporter of homeless and women's shelters in my local areas. Best of all I've been fortunate enough to help family members and friends in need.

Cherry on Top Moments:

- Being debt-free and financially secure
- Riding an elephant in Thailand, watching whales from a kayak in Maui, and taking a cooking class in Florence, Italy!
- Knowing that I can be there for my parents as they age
- New lifelong friendships
- Creating a legacy for my daughters
- Never having to worry about taking time off

From One Woman to Another: This industry is REAL! It's life changing. It's exhilarating. It's fun. When we treat it like a serious business, we can make SERIOUS money. The fact that we become successful by helping others fulfill their dreams is unique. There's no need to settle ... with this business, we CAN have it all!

Shauna Ekstrom Peterson

Age: 64
Lives: Grapevine, TX
Population: 52,000
Famliy: Married with 3 children
Number of Years as a Network Marketer: 20 years
Team Size: 377,000+
Highest Level of Education: Some High School, Cosmetology College

Before: Hairstylist for 34 years

Old Annual Income: $55,000

The Old Me: I was financially overwhelmed, in debt and spending more than I made. After 31 years of marriage, I was newly divorced and felt defined by my career as a hair stylist and salon owner. I missed far too many precious times with my 3 children while building my career.

My Four Year Career:

Looking For It / (Found Me)

A client invited me to a meeting and I went just to appease her. When I saw people just like me at this meeting enjoying time and financial freedom, I wanted it too. I didn't know how, but I believed that I could master the business, just as I had mastered hair styling through education and practice.

How I Heard of Network Marketing: I was approached many times over the years about Network Marketing, but I always said, "No, this isn't for me." I didn't really know what it was because I was approached by excited, well-meaning people who didn't explain the power of the business model. When I attended that first event, I got excited because I saw the true potential of residual income and I had to have it!

Move Over Ice Cream, Let's See the Real Deal:

YEAR ONE: The first month I enrolled 30 people. I used the products exactly as recommended and had a very visual physical transformation. I decided that a fast start was best to create momentum, and moved on to enroll 57 more in my first year. I still worked very full time at my salon, but my "side hustle" started to grow!

YEAR TWO: I worked closely with my friends and clients who joined me. Home meetings led to larger meetings. I sponsored 52 more people who loved the products. I was looking for a serious business partner to work hard at this with me, someone who needed this as much as I did. Joni Brewer joined me 21 months into my business. She became my running buddy, and things started heating up!

YEAR THREE: I was still working 60 hours a week at the salon and dedicating 3 hours a night to Network Marketing. I enrolled 48 more people and was earning 2x my annual income in hair with my Network Marketing business.

YEAR FOUR: My focus began to shift. I was able to go down to 20 hours a week at the salon, and I was spending 30 hours a week in Network Marketing. My team was growing exponentially, and I continued sponsoring 5 people per month. It wasn't long until I was able to sell my salon, free up a big chunk of my time, and transition into living my life by design!

Who I've Become: My posture and confidence in this business model is unwavering. Where I come from, my education, or lack thereof, does not define me. I have gone from working hard just to get by, to creating a seven-figure, legacy family business that includes my daughter.

Because I Said Yes, I Now: I no longer live in financial fear. You can't feed the poor by being one of them. By sharing my story, I get to help others start their own four year careers. I created a legacy business for myself and my family and have the privilege of showing others that they not only deserve this opportunity, but there's a system in place to accomplish their dreams.

Not only are we able to make a difference financially, but because of the flexibility this profession gives, we are able to donate our time to many people and causes.

Cherry on Top Moments:

- Becoming my company's 26th millionaire and my daughter (Heidi Poche) becoming our company's 125th millionaire!
- Meeting, marrying my husband, Dr. Scott F. Peterson, and getting to have a 7-week honeymoon! He retired from Dentistry and now we build this business side by side!
- Shopping with my grandkids without looking at price tags!
- Purchasing my mother's home.

From One Woman to Another: "The most expensive thing you'll ever own is a closed mind." Do your research. Grow into the person you want to attract. Seek out open, honest, hungry, and coachable partners. Add Network Marketing into your schedule, and work as if your life depends on it! And have fun!

This success story is not typical. It is an exceptional exception shared here to inspire you and show you what's possible. It is not what you should expect to accomplish.

Sonia Magruder

Lives: New Port Richey, FL
Population: 16,000
Famliy: Married with 3 stepsons
Number of Years as a Network Marketer: 4 years
Team Size: 21,000+
Highest Level of Education: High School

Before: Real estate agent, then broker with my own firm; real estate investor

Old Annual Income: Six figures

The Old Me: I was a very successful real estate broker and enjoyed what I did. While the money was great, I was on demand practically 24/7 and rarely had time to unplug and enjoy a vacation or even just some downtime with my family.

My Four Year Career:

Looking For It   / (Found Me)

My husband and I had an amazing product experience. People started asking us what we were doing, and we wanted to shout it from the rooftops because of the profound changes we experienced.

How I Heard of Network Marketing: My cousin Eric, who is a health nut, was posting his love for the products on his Facebook page. I approached him and asked him to tell me about them. I trusted him because of how meticulous he is about nutrition. After we had such great results, it naturally evolved into sharing, and very shortly became a monthly income equal to one of our rental properties.

Move Over Ice Cream, Let's See the Real Deal:

YEAR ONE: In the first 90 days I enrolled about 9 people. However, I saw things starting to duplicate, caught the vision, and went on to enroll around 40 people my first year.

YEAR TWO: My real estate income was replaced! We really got traction, and leader legs started to develop. We began to see the beauty of exponential growth.

YEAR THREE: My real estate income was surpassed, and leaders on our team started earning six figures, which was amazing.

YEAR FOUR: I have personally sponsored around 100 people, developed leaders, and my Network Marketing income has now surpassed my biggest year in real estate, but with time freedom!

Who I've Become: I thought I was a confident businessperson before, but this profession has helped me overcome fears that I had, especially public speaking. It has also helped me become more empathetic to people, become a better listener, and experience the gratification that comes from helping others succeed like never before. I love nothing more than mentoring and working with people who are motivated and who want success; it's my favorite part of this profession.

Because I Said Yes, I Now: I love seeing the greatness in others when they don't see it themselves and helping them cultivate their gifts. Helping people cast a vision and break mental patterns to change their mindset with empowering thoughts is magical. (Thank you, Richard Brooke.) I love helping others overcome their fears and seeing them go from fledglings to eagles. Being able to help families reduce their workloads so they can have more quality time with each other is incredible. Having the freedom to travel whenever we want and work from wherever we want is so much fun and truly a blessing.

Cherry on Top Moments:

- Overcoming my most dreaded fear, public speaking, to speaking in front of 1,000 people.
- Overcoming a 15-year phobia of flying when I had to go to our national convention across the country!
- Making incredible friends through this business who have become like family.

From One Woman to Another: Procrastination is expensive! Whatever your fear is, action will kill it and you will grow. Get into massive action like there's no tomorrow, and be consistent. Consistent daily actions will hit critical mass and pay off. Obstacles are guaranteed. Finding the opportunity in them—rather than quitting—leads to growth.

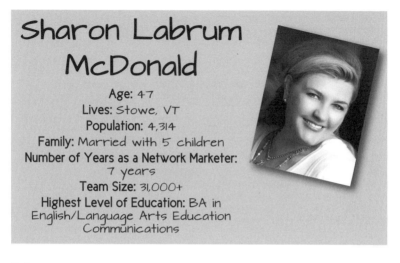

Sharon Labrum McDonald

Age: 47
Lives: Stowe, VT
Population: 4,314
Family: Married with 5 children
Number of Years as a Network Marketer: 7 years
Team Size: 31,000+
Highest Level of Education: BA in English/Language Arts Education Communications

Before: Full-time mom

Old Annual Income: My husband's six-figure income

The Old Me: I was your everyday woman with a desire to help women be their best ... not just at home, but in anything they pursued. I was keenly aware I needed to inspire women to riseUP; I just did not know how it would unfold.

My Four Year Career:

Looking For It / (Found Me)

I was open to my higher purpose, but it took my husband's invitation for me to look at Network Marketing as a profession.

How I Heard of Network Marketing: Many salespeople gave the wrong spiel to me. No one I knew was successful, and no one was professional; it was just a hobby. I did not want a hobby. Then my eyes were turned to what was possible and how to do this professionally. I decided it was something I should do well, and teach others to do equally well.

Move Over Ice Cream, Let's See the Real Deal:

YEAR ONE: I personally enrolled 45 people and hit our first major rank in the company.

YEAR TWO: I personally enrolled 30 more people and headed over to Europe to bring our company there. I had an annual income of $80K.

YEAR THREE: I personally enrolled another 15 people and put together systems for educating everyday people. I celebrated our second highest rank achievement. Two months later, I was diagnosed with breast cancer.

YEAR FOUR: I enrolled 10 people, however, my business came to a screeching halt. Luckily, my income did not! Personally, it was a year of recuperating and reconstruction. While I only enrolled about 8 people, my team continued to grow on its own. I started systemizing all processes to allow for duplication, and my annual income was $300K. I don't know any other profession that allows you to heal from illness the correct way and continues to pay you at the same time!

Who I've Become: I am able to work anywhere in the world with my family by my side. My passion to inspire others to be wildly confident has only grown deeper, as has my resolve that all things are possible. I know that nothing will stop me from helping others achieve their higher purpose and fulfill their mission ... not by MAKING IT HAPPEN, but through flow. When we align, it all happens. When we align with our purpose, doors open.

Because I Said Yes, I Now: I help others design lives of personal triumph and freedom, and I pay it forward by teaching others to do the same. Through that confidence, these women increase the faith and destiny of their children and leave a legacy of greatness for their families. Inspiring others to break old patterns and reach for better health while developing lives of strength and resolve fuels me to dig deeper and go further. I love giving back and going where we are called to go. It is fun to live by design, but seeing others you share with do the same ... PRICELESS!

Cherry on Top Moments:

- Clearing the glass ceiling for women.
- Furthering the development of women's leadership through speaking and writing opportunities.
- Traveling the world with my family; lifting others up wherever we go.
- Having my husband leave Corporate America because he saw the possibilities.
- Learning that EVERYONE can CHOOSE THEIR LIFE.

From One Woman to Another: Never stop believing. When doubt comes, squash it fast and discern where it is <u>really</u> coming from. We are destined to unite the world with our love and strength; it starts in our homes and flows into our communities. We just need to be brave and rise together, treating our business as a profession and not a hobby. If you are not serious with your daily activities, you will not meet your goals and attract the tribe that is waiting for you.

Judy O'Higgins

Age: 73
Lives: Cottonwood, AZ
Population: 11,000
Famliy: Widowed in 2017
Number of Years as a Network Marketer:
12 years
Team Size: 4,000
Highest Level of Education: Master of
Social Work Degree

Before: I had a 25-year career as a counselor/therapist, helping women to change and uplift their lives.

Old Annual Income: $50,000

The Old Me: I loved my career and empowering women to a better life. Toward the end, however, I experienced severe burnout. I knew I needed to retire, but financially I couldn't, because like so many baby boomers, I had not saved enough and felt trapped.

My Four Year Career:

Looking For It   / ⟨ Found Me ⟩

The month before I was introduced to my company, I had been very depressed and praying for a solution where I could retire from counseling but still help others in some way. My prayer was answered with a phone call from an old friend.

How I Heard of Network Marketing: My friend told me of a "little company that nobody's ever heard of, but I think it's going to be BIG" and encouraged me to try the product, which I LOVED. I signed up that night on faith and a credit card! When I met the founder and CEO and heard his vision for changing the world, I knew I was in the right place.

Move Over Ice Cream, Let's See the Real Deal:

YEAR ONE: In my first year of working part-time around my counseling schedule, my team grew to over 100, including 3 solid leaders who would go on to build key legs.

YEAR TWO: By the end of year two, my team was at 900 and growing. My residual income checks consistently had a comma in them for 6 months, and I was able to retire from my 25-year career.

YEAR THREE: By the end of year three, my team had grown to 3,000 and I had promoted myself 3 times, reaching a level that was in the top 1 percent of all company distributors.

YEAR FOUR: My team grew to 4,000 and my residual income checks kept going up. More leaders emerged and grew their own teams ... duplication! I could take time away from the business and it still grew without me!

Who I've Become: I have gone from someone who only felt confident inside my counseling office to a self-confident Network Marketer who has become comfortable speaking to groups, starting conversations with anyone, stepping into a leadership role, and becoming an author of 3 books (so far) related to Network Marketing. The personal growth aspect of this profession is profound!

Because I Said Yes, I Now: I now have total freedom to live where I choose, spend my time on my schedule and not someone else's, and let go of worrying about how the bills will get paid. I can travel, spend time with my friends, participate in causes I believe in, and still get paid every month! The past 2 years I had to take a "time out" from my business to take care of my husband when he became seriously ill. However, my business kept going without me after years of building it up! I can't stress enough what a miracle Network Marketing is to baby boomers who need additional income in retirement, not to mention inspiring others to take charge of their financial futures.

Cherry on Top Moments:

- Receiving my company's "Runner Up Distributor of the Year" award.
- Being a 6-time member of the Advisory Group to our CEO.
- Becoming a published author of 3 books on Network Marketing.
- Being a role model for others that you can be successful at any age with your own business, and it's never too late to go for your dreams.

From One Woman to Another: Do NOT let self-doubt hold you back. When someone offers you a great opportunity, say YES first, and then figure out the "how" later! You are just ONE decision away from changing your life. Don't wait!

_____
Your Name Here

Age: _____

Lives: _____

Population: _____

Family: _____

Highest Level of Education: _____

_____

Your Face Here

Go ahead, fill it out!

Yes, even what you will create over your Four Year Career!

You will be amazed at the things that happen in your life when you're willing to put them down on paper!

My Four Year Career:

Looking For It or Found Me?

_____

_____

How I Heard of Network Marketing:

_____

_____

Move Over Ice Cream, Let's See the Real Deal:

YEAR ONE:

_____

_____

YEAR TWO:

_____

_____

YEAR THREE:

_____

_____

YEAR FOUR:

_____

_____

Who I've Become (Describe your personality and who you are right now.):

_____

_____

Because I Said Yes, I Now (Who would you like to become and what charities would you like to contribute to?):

_____

_____

Cherry on Top Moments (What things would be amazing to experience that right now seem far out of reach or impossible? i.e.: buying my dream home, retiring my husband, building an orphanage ... whatever inspires you to dream!):

_____

_____

Keep this book and refer back to it throughout your Four Year Career to see what you manifested right here on these pages.

ABOUT KIMMY BROOKE

Kimmy Brooke watched heartbroken as her 11-year-old daughter, Hailey, boarded a plane to spend the summer with her aunt in Colorado. They had never been apart before. As a single parent, she knew she was making the right choice, but that didn't make it any easier. She wanted her daughter to have a fun summer, and Kimmy knew she had to put in long hours at work. Rent was expensive in Hawaii, and she was struggling to make ends meet. As her daughter's plane pulled away from the gate, Kimmy made a decision to do things differently. If she didn't, she would remain stuck. That's the day she turned life from lemons to lemonade and started to build her Four Year Career.

Today Kimmy is an entrepreneur, author, coach, trainer, and speaker. With no previous experience in Network Marketing, she went from zero to seven figures in less than four years and has traveled the world with her daughter. She is married to entrepreneur and bestselling author Richard Brooke, and together they run Bliss Business, a generic Network Marketing company that provides training materials, consulting, and support for Network Marketers from all companies. Kimmy's mission is to inspire and empower as many other women as possible by sharing her story. She works with Women United For Change, a movement in partnership with Project Concern International (PCI) to invest in women around the world.

By purchasing this book, you can help contribute to Kimmy's vision and commitment to empower women around the globe. She believes when women invest in each other, together they can change the world. With every copy sold, you can be a part of a powerful movement to help women in need. Recommend or pass this book on to a sister, mother, or bestie, and help change the lives of women worldwide.

ACKNOWLEDGEMENTS

How do you thank people who shape who you are and who you've become? Thank you doesn't begin to cover it, and I want to take the time to acknowledge those who I am grateful for every day. You are my tribe.

To Lisa Hemmeter and Katie Fredricksen, who opened the door to my new life; I am forever grateful.

To Jordan Adler, whose book *Beach Money* gave me the idea to meet with someone on my lunch break every day.

To my leaders, some who are still with me, some who are not. I think about each of you often and how much you have impacted my life.

To Sonia Stringer, Founder of Savvy Network Marketing Women

Josephine and Chris Gross, Founders of *Networking Times*

Marina and Eric Worre, Founders of Network Marketing Pro

Lory Muirhead and Janine Finney, Authors of *The Flip Flop CEO*

Randy Gage and Art Jonak, Co-Founders of The Mastermind Event

Each of your contributions to my growth in the profession has been profound. Thank you for helping me share my gifts with a bigger audience.

To Melissa Gulbranson, my biggest cheerleader and advocate. I cannot imagine doing this work without your support.

To Melissa Fullam. Thank you for your hours upon hours of dedication to this project and holding the space for it to keep getting better. This really is "our" book.

To my tribe of women, because everyone needs a tribe. You know who you are, and I love you.

To my incredible family. My mom and dad, Bobbie, Kirsten, Lisa, Mark, Taylor, Maddy, and Annabelle. There's a piece of each of you responsible for who I am today.

To Hailey, I'm not sure if you are aware of how much you continuously influence my life choices. In everything I do, every decision I make, you are right there, in my mind. I realize the success of my business has meant sacrifices on your part. The late night meetings, travel time away, and calls while driving you to school were all prices for the life we have created.

I'm far from perfect, but know my intention has always been to provide you with an extraordinary life. I want to thank you for being the driving force that has me always wanting to push myself to be more. There is no love as strong as my love for you.

To Richard, you were the puzzle piece that was missing from our lives. Without you, there wouldn't have been a reason or inspiration to write this.

Thank you for your generosity and willingness to share your brand and idea with me to help serve even more people. You are the King of all Kings.

And to all who were, and will be, brave enough to say YES to their very own Four Year Careers. It's because of you I wrote this book.